Designing for User Engagement

Aesthetic and Attractive User Interfaces

Synthesis Lectures on Human-Centered Informatics

Editor

John M. Carroll, Edward M. Frymoyer Professor of Information Sciences and Technology,
Penn State University

Designing for User Engagement: Aesthetic and Attractive User Interfaces
Alistair Sutcliffe

ISBN: 978-3-031-01060-6   paperback
ISBN: 978-3-031-02188-6   ebook

DOI 10.1007/978-3-031-02188-6

A Publication in the Springer series
SYNTHESIS LECTURES ON HUMAN-CENTERED INFORMATICS

Lecture #5
Series Editor: John M. Carroll, Edward M. Frymoyer Professor of Information Sciences and Technology, Penn State University
Series ISSN
Synthesis Lectures on Human-Centered Informatics
Print 1946-7680   Electronic 1946-7699

Designing for User Engagement

Aesthetic and Attractive User Interfaces

Alistair Sutcliffe
University of Manchester

SYNTHESIS LECTURES ON HUMAN-CENTERED INFORMATICS #5

ABSTRACT

This book explores the design process for user experience and engagement, which expands the traditional concept of usability and utility in design to include aesthetics, fun and excitement. User experience has evolved as a new area of Human Computer Interaction research, motivated by non-work oriented applications such as games, education and emerging interactive Web 2.0. The chapter starts by examining the phenomena of user engagement and experience and setting them in the perspective of cognitive psychology, in particular motivation, emotion and mood. The perspective of aesthetics is expanded towards interaction and engagement to propose design treatments, metaphors, and interactive techniques which can promote user interest, excitement and satisfying experiences. This is followed by reviewing the design process and design treatments which can promote aesthetic perception and engaging interaction. The final part of the chapter provides design guidelines and principles drawn from the interaction and graphical design literature which are cross-referenced to issues in the design process. Examples of designs and design treatments are given to illustrate principles and advice, accompanied by critical reflection.

KEYWORDS

user experience, user engagement, aesthetics, new usability, guidelines, design quality

Contents

CHAPTER 1

Introduction

This chapter addresses design for attractive and engaging user interfaces while forming part of the new design agenda usually called User Experience. The term user experience (UX) has grown out of concerns that traditional concepts of usability [39, 60] did not cover the more aesthetic aspects of design. Traditionally, usability has emphasized ease of use, ease of learning and effective operation, in other words, the 'drivability of an interface' and how well it fits the user's task and goals. Norman questioned the traditional view of usability in his book on emotion in design [52] and pointed to the importance of aesthetics aspects in user interfaces and users' emotional responses to well designed products. Other critiques of traditional usability come from product design [31], in which design goals related to pleasure and aesthetic appeal are considered to be as important as efficiency and effectiveness. Researchers in Human Computer Interaction (HCI) began to question how aesthetic design might be related to usability, led by the pioneering studies of Tractinsky who experimentally manipulated usability and aesthetic qualities of a design to coin the now well known aphorism "what is beautiful is usable" [43, 69]. This referred to compensations which users appear to make when judging product quality: they are prepared to forgive poor usability in more aesthetic versions of products. Subsequent research has shown the 'beautiful is usable' phenomenon to be more complex and context-dependent [33, 64].

User experience also evolved from marketing concepts such as "consumer experience" [68] which refers to the totality of product experience including sales, set up, use, support during use, maintenance, etc. While UX is the more general term, "user engagement" has a more restricted sense that focuses on the quality of the interactive experience rather than the whole life span experience of a product. Other influences came from research into enjoyment and fun [8] and application areas such as games and entertainment where traditional usability appeared to be less appropriate. When excitement and amusement are the major design goals, interaction, metaphor and aesthetics become important concerns. Hence, in HCI, user engagement and experience generally refer to a wider concept of design beyond functional products, which encompasses interaction, flow [17], and aesthetic design. It draws on literature from psychology, investigating how people assess aesthetically related design qualities [32, 33, 34], interaction and graphical design [30, 59] and contextual analysis of interaction [23, 46].

This chapter has three aims. First, I will introduce the concepts of user engagement, and I will relate them to aesthetic design and more traditional approaches in HCI anchored in usability. Secondly, I will describe techniques and processes which contribute to UE design, and finally, I will review some of the design principles and guidelines which are oriented towards UE.

CHAPTER 2

Psychology of User Engagement

User experience is a concept which is frequently discussed but not easy to define. Indeed, UX has been associated with a wide variety of meanings, ranging from traditional usability to beauty, hedonic, and affective and experiential aspects of technology use [29, 36]. The ISO 13407 revised draft definition [38] gives a rather anodyne view that UX is "A person's perceptions and responses that result from the use or anticipated use of a product, system or service". Law et al. [44] give no fewer than five definitions which they used in a survey of academics and industrial designers. One of the two most popular definitions in their survey was "The consequence of a user's internal state (predispositions, expectations, needs, motivations, mood, etc.), the characteristics of the designed system (e.g., complexity, purpose, usability, functionality, etc.) and the context (or the environment) within which the interaction occurs (e.g., organizational/social setting)". The second most popular definition emphasized the effect and affect produced by aesthetic experience, the meaning we attach to the product, and the feelings and emotions produced. Wikipedia defines UX and user experience design as a subset of the field of experience design that "pertains to the creation of the architecture and interaction models that impact a user's perception of a device or system" and borrows Norman's view that UX pertains to "all aspects of the user's interaction with the product: how it is perceived, learned, and used". UX, therefore, includes usability and perceptions of utility, but it goes further to consider emotional responses.

A definition closer to the marketing concept is "the totality of user experience from acquiring, customizing and configuring an interactive product, through learning and use, including maintenance and modification, ending in product disposal". However, for this chapter, I will focus on design and the user's experience, so a more restricted definition is appropriate: "user's judgement of product quality arising from their experience of interaction, and the product design qualities while engender effective use and pleasure". In accordance with my definition, I will approach UX from two directions, first from the user's judgement of their experience and, secondly, from the design perspective to enquire which features or qualities might deliver a high-quality user experience. At this stage, I will add a word warning. Many in the design community would argue that design guidelines can not be articulated; instead, excellent design quality leading to satisfying user experiences can only be produced by several years of mentoring and experientially led design education. In terms of the upper bound of design quality, I would agree; however, for the majority of user interface designers and software developers, understanding user experience and articulating guidance on how to achieve it are realizable and worthwhile goals. That is what this chapter aims to provide.

Since UX is a diffuse and much over-used term, I will propose "user engagement" (UE) to describe how people are attracted to use interactive products. User engagement will be reserved primarily to explain how and why applications attract people to use them within a session and make interaction exciting and fun while UX will be reserved for the wider picture covering why people adopt and continue to use a particular design over many sessions and even years.

2.1 AESTHETICS AND USER JUDGEMENT

Norman's focus on emotion and affect [52] created a partial red herring in understanding UE. Emotions are reactions to events, objects, and even memories , which invoke psychosomatic responses [53], so while they are a component of understanding UE, a more important focus lies in understanding human judgement. There have been two approaches to this. The first has been a quest to understand the deep-seated constructs by which we make judgments about product quality. The second takes a more process-oriented view to understand how we make quality-related judgments. Tractinsky developed questionnaires for measuring user judgments about the quality of interactive products, producing measures for classical and expressive aesthetics, traditional usability and pleasure [43]. However, when the determinants of classic aesthetics are inspected, many relate to traditional usability concepts such as consistency and structural layout, so the expressive aesthetics and pleasure scales are better reflections of UE. Hassenzahl took a similar questionnaire-based approach but investigated the underlying constructs in more detail, proposing hedonic and pragmatic design qualities and, more recently, the interplay between goodness and hedonic qualities [34, 35, 36]. Perception of hedonic qualities is more closely associated with aesthetics, and pragmatics is closer to traditional usability, while the role of goodness is unclear. However, these studies tend to ignore the fact that user judgement is context-dependent, as cognitive theories of judgement and decision making demonstrate [54, 55]. So whatever the underlying constructs by which we judge products, our judgement depends on the context of use.

Evidence for this process-oriented view comes for a series of studies I have conducted with colleagues using Tractinsky's questionnaires to assess websites and interactive products which share the same functionality and content but differ in aesthetic and interaction design [33]. We showed that user judgement can be biased by the tasks they are given (serious v. less serious use) [19, 64], by their background and task [32], and by the order in which design information (positive/negative) is presented [33]. These studies drew on well known effects in psychology: the halo effect by which judgement of one quality can spill over into another [21], framing and priming effects by which judgement is influenced by prior provision of information, and even the order in which positive or negative expression of the same information is presented [7]. So "what is beautiful is usable" depends on the context, and the reverse can also be true when users are given serious tasks; moreover, judgement of the same website can be swayed by the order in which the same information is given. Clearly, beauty is in the eye of the beholder, but it depends on who the beholder is and what they are doing. User judgement of user experience is, therefore, a complex process, which is summarized in Fig. 2.1. This elaborates adaptive decision making theory [54] to include the criteria by which people may make quality judgments and how the sequence of interaction will influence judgement criteria.

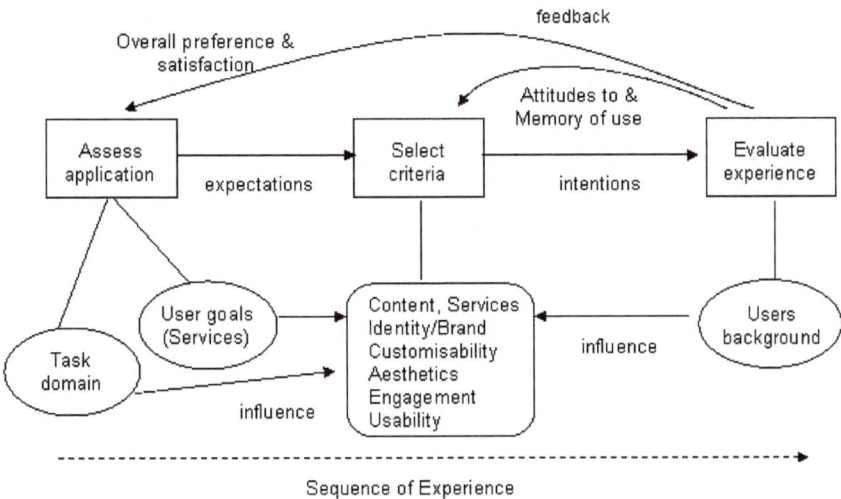

Figure 2.1: Elaboration of adaptive decision making theory [54] for design quality judgement of inter-active products.

On initial encounter, users assess the application according to their goals and the task domain. This stage will correspond to searching and locating a website or a software product. Next, the users' goals and task influence the selection of the decision-making criteria. For example, in applications for serious use with more critical outcomes, content and usability will be favoured. Alternatively, for less serious use (e.g., entertainment, games), aesthetics and engagement will be favoured. The user's experience will be judged against the dominant criterion or criteria appropriate for the application. The decision-making process is iterative, and users modify their opinions as their experience progresses. UE is, therefore, a complex multifaceted quality which may vary according to the application, the users' expectations and context of use. For example, in work/goal-oriented applications, functionality, utility and usability are going to be more important. When applications are mobile, adaptation and context sensitivity will be important: while if the brand is valued, this exerts a positive influence on other criteria such as usability and aesthetics [9]. For power users, the ability to customize and adapt the application will be key criteria. In contrast, for games and entertainment aesthetics, metaphors and interaction may be dominant. The correspondence between judgement criteria and applications types, as well as user characteristics, is still largely un-researched, so few definitive guidelines can be given.

To make a complex picture even worse, the criteria people use to make judgments probably shift as experience progresses. For initial impressions, aesthetics may be important, but as interaction commences, usability and utility will dominate in task-oriented applications while action-feedback, presence and metaphors are probably more important in games and entertainment domains. Experience is evaluated, resulting in positive or negative attitudes which feed back on the criteria. However, feedback involves a complex interaction between the dominant and non-dominant criteria, the task, and user background, all of which influence overall preference. Cognitive models of user judgement point out that we sometimes make judgement by 'gut reaction' or fast-path processing, involving little reflective thinking. In serious contexts, we make judgments more slowly with elaborate thinking, the slow path [55]. Work domains are more likely to involve slow-path decisions and usability/utility criteria whereas entertainment domains are more likely to be based on fast-path judgement. Fast-path judgments are frequently based on memory and "gut feeling"; furthermore, our memorized experiences are frequently made more vivid by emotion. So Norman's red herring [52] did have a point. Emotion fits into decision making and may become an important influence on our judgement. Excitement, surprise and pleasure are the positive emotions closely related to flow and interaction design, and I shall concentrate on this perspective in the design sections of this chapter. However, before turning to design we need to complete our understanding of the role of psychology.

2.2   AFFECT, AROUSAL AND ENGAGEMENT

The cognition behind UE is summarized in Fig. 2.2. Emotion influences judgement, but judgement and experience from interaction also affect our emotions and memory. We remember events after

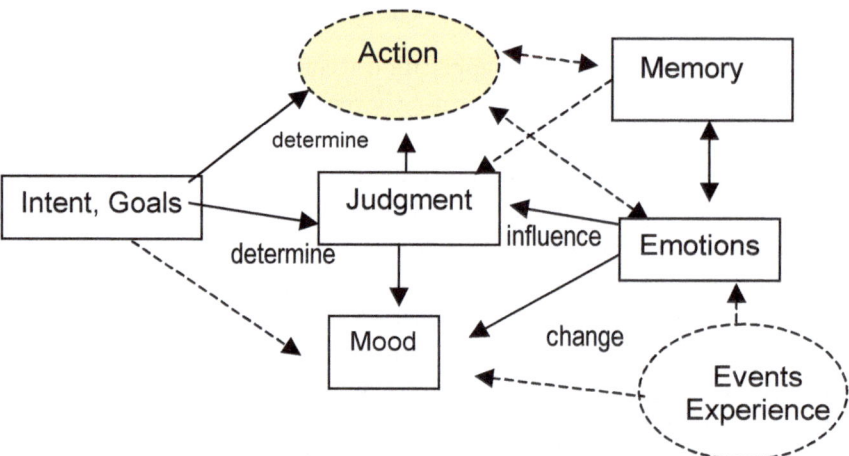

Figure 2.2: Model of cognitive factors influencing UE.

unpleasant incidents more effectively than events beforehand (proactive inhibition). Unpleasant events become highly salient memories, but proactive inhibition often suppresses what led up to the event, making eyewitness testimony unreliable [1]. A bad usability experience will trigger emotions of frustration, anxiety and even anger. Since negative emotions tend to enhance memory of the situations and the immediate episode that gave rise to them, poor usability will be remembered and associated with the product in the future. Design qualities such as good aesthetics and usability are likely to evoke positive emotions, such as pleasure and joy, leading to positive memories, although we tend to remember positive experiences in more general terms. We have found that a positive usability experience was not remembered in any detail but poor usability was while general impressions of good aesthetic design were remembered favorably [19, 64], so it appears that usability has to avoid serious errors while investing in aesthetics adds value.

Emotions interact with the arousal mechanism, which can be considered as a dimension ranging from calmness to excitement [6]. Interaction, unexpected events, unusual and unpleasant stimuli all tend to increase arousal, and high arousal increases the strength of emotional experience. Our feelings are a combination of arousal and emotion that persist as a mood, which may last for hours and possibly days and affect our judgement. Pleasing and enjoyable user experience will produce a positive mood; in contrast, poor design, errors and difficulties could leave us in a bad mood, and bad moods may be reflected in future judgement of the product and related products.

2.3   AROUSAL, ENGAGEMENT AND FLOW

Arousal and emotion play an important role in UE. High quality aesthetic design will evoke pleasure and mild arousal; however, interaction is probably a more important influence. We have to pay attention when we act; furthermore, action, attention and concentration all increase our arousal [49]. Interaction inevitably means we have to concentrate on deciding how to act, and on evaluating the consequences of our action as succinctly summarized in Norman's action and gulfs models [51]. Concentration is our ability to attend to a user interface or any task over a significant period of time; however, the strength of its influence depends on the difficulty of the task in hand and our previous experience. Rasmussen's KRS (Knowledge, Rules, Skills) model [57] provides a useful framework that links judgement, problem solving, action, and experience. When we encounter a user interface for the first time and it is unfamiliar, we decide how to act using general common sense knowledge or heuristics. This is the knowledge level and involves slow-path judgement. A typical heuristic is trial and error, e.g., push a few buttons and see what happens. More often, we have some idea about the UI, so we apply previous knowledge to plan our actions. In Rasmussen's framework, this is the rule level where we apply declarative knowledge (if-then rules) to predict how to act. The HCI consistency principle is motivated by the rule level: if we can apply a general rule across different applications then we can guess how to operate any consistent user interface. We apply rules to guess how to pull down menus, toggle button settings, or close windows by the X icon in the top right-hand corner. Finally, when we are completely familiar with an application, we apply skilled knowledge, as precompiled procedures that we run automatically, and fast-path decision making. Driving a car is a good example for most of us. Skilled operation is the least arousing of the KRS levels since we do not have to do much active thinking; hence, we find skilled, repetitive tasks boring. The rule and knowledge levels are more arousing since we have to reason more actively. Games designers know this intuitively. Nearly all games which are based on skilled operation have levels of difficulty which can be set by the user or automatically, to avoid the game getting boring once simple skilled operation has been mastered.

The challenge in user engagement is to hold the user's interest and maintain arousal by interaction which varies in difficulty and familiarity between Rasmussen's levels. In work/goal-oriented applications, skilled operation and efficiency will be more important; hence, ease of learning and ease of use are paramount. But in entertainment and education domains, interaction that promotes arousal for engagement will be more important. This leads us to the concept of flow [17].

FLOW

Flow is the sense of engagement and being absorbed in an interactive experience. The concept involves optimal arousal produced by a 'sweet spot' trade-off between challenge and difficulty on one hand and ease of operation and achievement on the other. If operating a UI is too difficult, we will get frustrated and discouraged and may give up, leaving us with negative emotions and adverse memory of the experience. In contrast, if operating the UI is too easy, then we get bored, excitement (or arousal) decreases, and we turn our attention to more interesting things. The trick is to keep interaction in the flow zone (see Fig. 2.3), an intuition appreciated by game designers. Games need

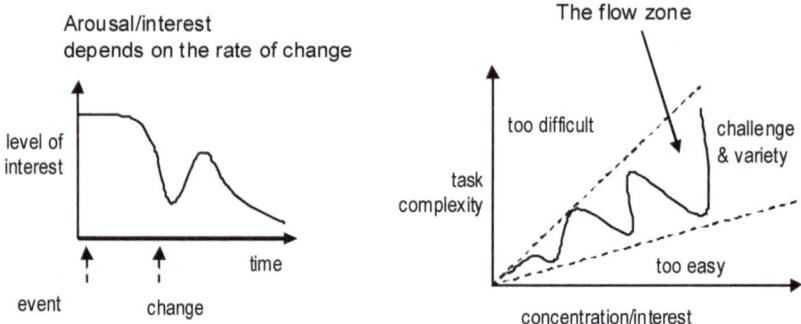

Figure 2.3: Change in arousal as events become familiar; and the concept of flow.

to maintain the pace of change with unpredictable events while not overwhelming the user with too much change that exceeds their capabilities. We rapidly get used to patterns of events leading to decreased arousal as the unfamiliar becomes familiar.

Games manipulate the flow of events to maintain a sufficient level of engagement and difficulty, by scripting surprises and varying the behaviour of other agents, usually the enemy in the first-person shooter genre of games [37]. Sophisticated games monitor the user's behaviour and success rate and adapt the level of difficulty to maintain flow; less sophisticated versions provide a skill re-set control so the user can increase the difficulty of level as required. However, there is more to engagement than just interaction; arousal and flow are also influenced by the sense of presence.

ENGAGEMENT AND PRESENCE

The origins of presence come from Virtual Reality (VR), in which the user is represented by an avatar or virtual character. The avatar places the user inside a 3D graphic world, so interaction becomes very different from operating an interface through a cursor. Presence is the sense of 'being there' inside a virtual world as a representation of yourself (embodied or immersed interaction). Embodied interaction is more complex than standard 2D interfaces since you can control movement directly, manipulate objects in an almost natural manner, and even feel objects if haptic feedback is provided. The sense of immersion and control is enhanced via natural movement. Hand movements in the real world can be replicated by glove tracking devices and represented faithfully in the virtual world, leading to the illusion that we are present and acting in the virtual world (see Fig. 2.4). Virtual worlds become engaging because they invoke curiosity and arousal; it is clearly not reality but a close enough copy to be predictable. Interaction becomes transparent, i.e., you are not aware of the computer, instead you feel immersed and become absorbed in the virtual graphical world.

Figure 2.4: Virtual world illustrating the user's presence represented as two virtual hands.

Interaction in virtual worlds can be explained in terms of flow. When the illusion of the virtual world is well designed, then you feel immersed with a strong sense of presence. Interaction thus feels as if you are in the real world since the computer essentially disappears. When the design is flawed, for example, tracking is too slow so the graphical world judders as you move, cognitive dissonance intervenes, and you become aware of the user interface as the illusion of the virtual world disappears, just as much as the illusion in a theatre vanishes when an actor forgets their lines. Presence is a tricky concept to measure although there are questionnaire checklists for that purpose [66, 71]; however, these do not capture subtle differences in presence which can depend on several aspects such as the viewpoint, avatar realism, controls for action, and modalities for feedback. For example, presence can be changed between exogenous views (when you are looking into the virtual world, and you can see your avatar) and endogenous views (set inside the virtual world as if you are surrounded by, or immersed in, the virtual world). Lack of haptic feedback and the sophistication of actions are the main limitations of presence and engagement in virtual worlds. Fortunately, we don't always need the expense of VR technology to achieve a sense of presence. Desktop VR, where you look into the 3D world on a PC with limited controls provided by a joystick, mouse or Wii device, provides very engaging and absorbing interaction.

ENGAGEMENT AND THE COMPUTER AS SOCIAL ACTOR

Strange as it may seem, it takes very little to create an illusion of presence. Our powerful imaginations just need a few hints (priming or framing effects in psychology) to conjure up a perceived reality, as Pinter and other proponents of minimalist theatre have demonstrated. Reeves and Nass in a series of experiments showed how we treat computer-based media as if they corresponded to real people. Their Computer as Social Actor (CSA) paradigm [58] explains how we treat computers as virtual people even when we are presented with limited cues, such as a photograph of a person or human voice. Indeed, the image can be artificial, cartoon-like, with little correspondence to reality; and the same applies to the voice. Chatterbots, avatars on the web equipped with simple semi intelligent scripts for responding to human conversations, are treated like real characters and some people actually form relationships with these virtual characters [18].

Images showing people's eyes and gaze attract attention while faces which fill the screen (close-ups) are more powerful attractors; however, large screens with close-up faces can be intimidating (Big Brother effect). In dialogue, praise and flattery by a computer is just as effective as being flattered in real life. There are many other human transference effects in the Media Equation [58]. The effect probably works because interaction and language are closely integrated, and we load a set of assumptions governing conversation whenever we are in the presence of people [15]. According to Clark's discourse theory of language, we interpret meaning by reference to the setting of the conversation and what we know about the other party; hence, there is a strong predisposition to attend to stimuli, suggesting human conversation and even photographs of people and to treat those stimuli by the same rules of conversation that we apply in real life, e.g., being praised by another induces a positive emotion of pleasure and attribution that the other person is nice. Gaze means pay attention, but it can also be threatening (see Fig. 2.5).

The CSA effect creates engagement because conversation is an important part of our life. Dialogue is fluid, changes rapidly and requires rule- and knowledge-based processing, so it stimulates engagement. We also spend a considerable part of our lives conversing, chatting and gossiping just to maintain social relationships [25], so the predisposition to be engaged in, and engaged by, conversation is probably deeply anchored in our evolutionary past. CSA also affects presence as we

Figure 2.5: Good example of the use of human face and gaze to attract attention.

assume a virtual human presence associated with the computer media conveying human images or voice.

ENGAGEMENT AND SOCIAL PRESENCE

Social presence theory [61] argues that different communication channels and representations promote more or less sense of social presence, i.e., awareness of the identity, location and personalities of other people. The theory does not give a formal classification or model of social presence although it can be re-interpreted in terms of CSA and models of communication channels which describe degradations from the ideal of Face-to-face (FTF), co-located communication. Evaluation criteria for communication channels from Brennan and Clark [10] can be used to assess computer-mediated communication (CMC) technologies in decreasing order of social presence; see Table 2.1. Video conferencing approaches the social presence of FTF, but even multi-camera views with sophisticated controls do not give us the same ability to scan a group of people to concentrate on the person who is speaking while also monitoring everyone else to see if they are attending, decide when to take a turn, etc.

e-Mail as an asynchronous conversation is the least engaging since the time gap between turns destroys the sense of a dialogue, whereas instant messaging (IM) approaches synchronous exchange and become more engaging. In IM, the pace of exchange approaches a conversation and the sense of presence increases. Adding video or even still images improves presence by providing more information about the other person (see Fig. 2.6). However, e-mail and text messages are persistent, so they can be reviewed and revised, and thereby support communication by a history of conversation.

Table 2.1: Communication channels (after [10]) and presence in CMC technologies.

Property	Media Example
Co-presence	Face-to-face
Visibility (modality)	Video conference (+audio)
Audibility (modality)	Phone
Contemporaneous (synchronous)	Chat IM
Simultaneous (synchronous)	Chat IM
Sequential (asynchronous)	e-Mail, texting (SMS)
Reviewable (messages)	e-Mail, text messages + images (not speech)
Revisable (messages)	e-Mail, text + image (not speech)

Figure 2.6: Second Life illustrating avatars which represent the characters people adopt and the location with others, both of which promote social presence.

Building on Clark's intuition about the importance of context in interpreting meaning and the concept of a dialogue as an integrated set of exchanges over time, social presence can be provided by a communication channel, and contextual information which gives us the background to an ongoing conversation. Conversation can be via speech or text and allow synchronous exchanges. The context may be provided by a user profile, a room or whatever has been constructed in the virtual world for interpreting the conversation. As interaction progresses, repeated meetings help build up knowledge about the identity of others, leading to social relationships

Social Networking Sites (SNS), such as Facebook, promote social presence more actively by making the conversational setting visible. When we engage in conversation with someone we know, we load an extensive memory about them to help us understand what they are saying, i.e., who they are, what they do, who their friends are, etc. Facebook helps our memory by displaying this information on demand (friend's profile, friends list), in the context of a conversation (wall, wall posts, private messaging) with added media (photo and video sharing). Facebook also augments our knowledge by awareness updates (newsfeeds) and facilitates multi-channel conversations, so I can send a private message to my friends, post comments on their wall, share photos, poke them, send them virtual gifts, throw virtual snowballs at them and indulge in an ever-growing set of interactive applications. All these interactions are conversations of a sort ranging from the slow-running asynchronous to fast, fluid and synchronous. Providing I have sufficient hours in the day to indulge in social networking, social mediating technologies provide new horizons for engagement. The success of immersive social worlds such as Second Life can be attributed to the sense of presence and engagement afforded by interacting in a 3D virtual world with avatar characters. The avatars, rooms, buildings or whatever that have been implemented on the user's island provide the context for the conversation. Thus, Second Life affords engaging interaction via presence in the interactive and social sense.

2.4 SUMMARY: THE PSYCHOLOGY OF ENGAGEMENT

User engagement is a complex concept that synthesizes several influences to promote a sense of flow and fluid interaction leading to satisfying arousal and pleasurable emotions of curiosity, surprise, and joy. The contributing influences are summarized in Fig. 2.7.

The three main components of user engagement are *interaction*, *media* and *presence*. Interaction describes the content being communicated. Media describes how the user and the means of interaction are represented, ranging from simple cursors to icons and interactive avatars. Presence is determined by the representation of the user and how immersion is afforded by the interface on a 2D interactive surface or in a more elaborate 3D interactive world. Presence is also related to, and augmented by, interaction. Acting in a 3D world and interaction with objects all increase the sense of being there and arousal. Flow is the key concept for understanding interaction in terms of the pace of action, complexity of actions and the rate of change. Flow, as explained earlier, is a finely tuned balancing act between the user's abilities and skills, and the challenges provided by learning new interactions and then responding to events within time limits and other resource constraints.

The expanded view of presence into the social dimension is illustrated in Fig. 2.8. Social presence is supported by the identity and character of the other party as conveyed by their representation.

Social and personal identity is also afforded by background information about the individual's interests, list of friends, and previous interactions. The contribution of background to social presence

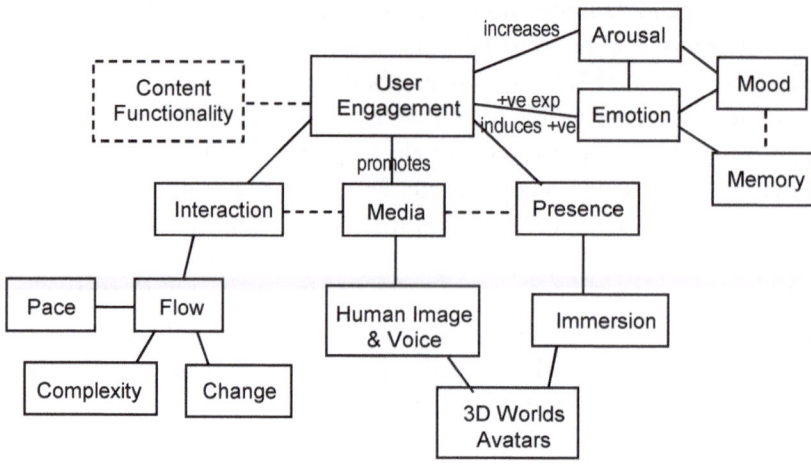

Figure 2.7: Influences contributing to user engagement, excluding social presence.

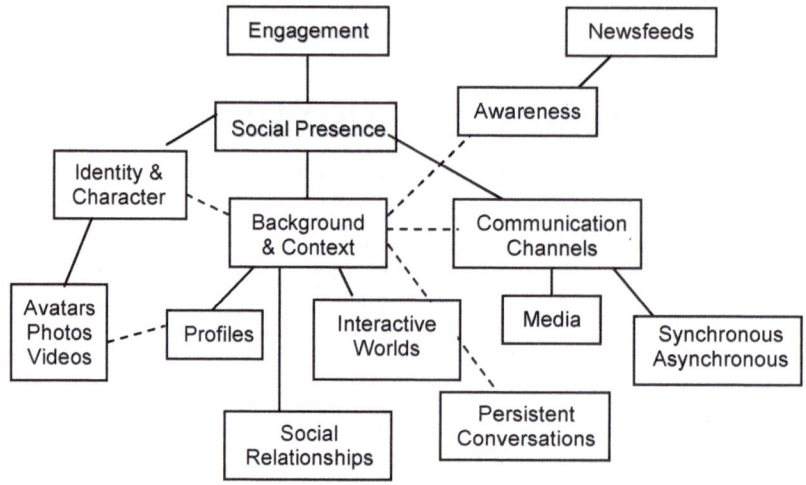

Figure 2.8: Social presence and engagement.

is augmented by information in the users' profiles, their social relationships, the settings within which they interact and the history of previous (persistent) conversations. Social presence is mediated more or less effectively by communication channels; furthermore, as the number and diversity of channels available in SNSs increases, technology is providing a richer sense of social presence. Finally, social presence is mediated by awareness functions such as newsfeeds which allow people to update their knowledge of others as well as simple 'I am on line' functions such as pokes.

User engagement and presence are, therefore, complex topics with several interacting components. How these components interact and how much they contribute to the overall sense of users' engagement and presence will depend on the interaction context, the user and other environmental factors such as time pressure and the application domain. Considerable further research is required to validate the above models, let alone espouse laws about which factors might be more important in which domains. However, the models do provide a more elaborate perspective for considering the criteria by which we make judgments about the attractiveness of applications (see Section 2.1).

USER ENGAGEMENT AND USER EXPERIENCE

The section commenced by trying to narrow the scope of UE so I will conclude by returning to the wider picture, having unpacked user engagement. As noted earlier (see Sectionch2.sec1) there are several criteria which may be loaded to shape users' judgments of attractiveness (see Fig.1.9).

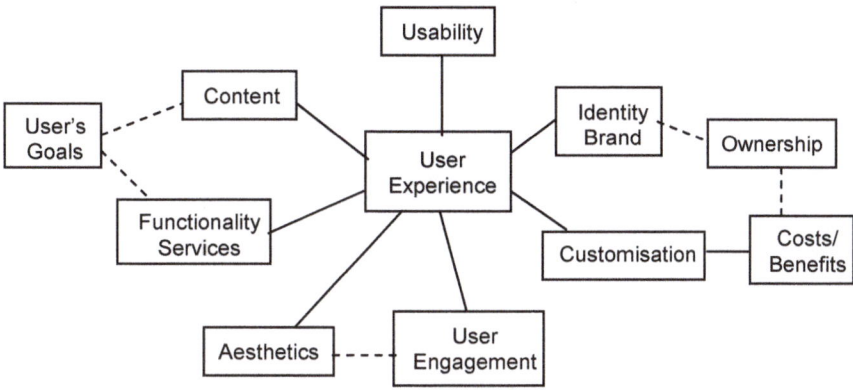

Figure 2.9: Components of user experience which may affect user judgement.

The weighting of the criteria will depend on the domain, the user's preferences and previous experience with similar applications. The attractiveness of content and functionality forms part of the wider view of UE. Content and functionality will be highly motivating if they are closely matched to the user's interests and goals. However, I am not elaborating this point beyond stressing that content and functionality are closely related to task goals, so these criteria will be more important in work-related applications. In contrast, engagement and aesthetics may gain importance in entertainment and leisure applications.

Customization is slightly different since this criterion is inherently multi-sessional and depends on the user's commitment to a design. I will finesse the debate about adaptivity v. adaptation (see [26]) in which either the application tries to automatically adapt to the user, or the user does the configuration/customization themselves (adaptation). Assuming user-driven adaptation/customization, the trade-off is between the user investing effort in configuring the application and the rewards of a better fit between the application and the user's needs. If the reward pays off, UE is enhanced not only through more stimulating interaction and better fit to the user's task and abilities [65] but also through the sense of ownership. Having devoted effort to configuring and hence changing the application, I have imposed my own, albeit limited, imprint on the product. Hence, to some degree, I feel ownership. This motivation can be enhanced by providing more extensive configuration facilities, leading to tools for end-user development and meta-design [27]; however, analysing user experience in the design process is beyond the scope of this chapter. Finally, usability is always important, but the ease of use required will depend on the domain, varying between high quality usability when content and functionality are priorities, to sufficient usability when user engagement and fun are the main criteria.

Having surveyed the concepts of UE and users' engagement with their constituents, I move in the next section to the process perspective and propose techniques and methods for engagement design.

CHAPTER 3

UE Design Process

There is no single accepted process for UE design; however, several approaches have been proposed for user-centred and participatory design of interactive products which attempt to stimulate creative design thinking. The approaches share techniques such as scenarios, mockups, storyboards and prototypes which provide quick realizations of designs that can be tested with users to explore their reactions [11, 16]. In common with other user-centred approaches, UE design needs to understand the user's requirements and then come up with solutions. Ideally, users should participate in the design process and contribute ideas and solutions themselves, thus helping to engage them in the design process and hence increase their sense of ownership of the design. When analysing users' requirements, the judgement criteria described in Chapter 2 provide useful probes to explore users' views of the application and their priorities for the product.

Scenario-based design [13] is a suitable approach for UE design since it advocates the use of scenarios, storyboards (screen mockups) and prototypes in an iterative cycle of requirements elicitation, design exploration and user feedback. This rapid iterative approach to development is shared by context analysis using ethnography [41], rapid application development methods (e.g., [24]) and, agile development methods [3]. Scenario-based design (SBD) integrates usability engineering within requirements analysis by applying HCI design principles in the form of psychological design rationales or claims. SBD is well suited to the challenges of UE because of its iterative approach, which facilitates user-developer dialogue by a combination of scenarios to illustrate users' experience, storyboards for design explorations, and claims to record the arguments for and against a particular design.

SCENARIOS

Scenarios are specific, realistic descriptions of user experience with applications. Scenarios are similar to stories in agile methods [3], which also provide examples and narratives describing events and experiences of use, either gathered directly from real life or invented as realistic visions of future designs. An example scenario is illustrated in the following example.

> Emma is doing a biology project on the impact of living conditions on health in the Stocksbridge area. She surfs the web and finds the Stocksbridge authority website. She would like to find statistics about health and lifestyles and any information that explains the link between them. She follows links on the Stocksbridge website. She notices that heart disease is one of the largest single causes of death in the UK. Furthermore, it is linked to lifestyle problems. She has some knowledge about how the heart works from her biology classes but doesn't know how heart disease is caused, nor why the causes

might be linked to smoking, poor exercise, etc. However, she can't find links to this information.

Scenarios are lightweight instruments that guide thought and support reasoning in the design process [13]. They may record past examples of good and bad user experience or present visions of future experiences. Carroll has articulated several different roles for scenarios in the design process including a 'cognitive prosthesis' to stimulate the designer's imagination, envisionment for design exploration, requirements elicitation and validation [14]. Other roles are usage scenarios, which illustrate problems; initiating or envisioning scenarios, which stimulate design of a new artefact; and projected use scenarios, which describe future use of an artefact that has been designed [63].

One limitation of scenarios is a potential bias towards exceptional and rare events, or towards the viewpoint of an unrepresentative stakeholder. These biases are an acknowledged weakness of scenarios; however, some propose scenarios with 'extreme characters' that are deliberately exceptional to provoke constructive thought [22]. Scenarios contribute to several parts of the design process. Task models, storylines and scripts come from a process of generalization across many scenarios that inevitably loses detail and the analyst has to make judgments about when unusual or exceptional behaviours are omitted. Scenarios also contribute contextual information for interpretation of user requirements and their priorities (see judgement criteria) for the design, especially in combination with personae.

PERSONAE

Personae are character sketches of typical users and user roles. An example is

Emma is a high-school student, age 16. She comes from a well-to-do background and is well motivated at school. So far she has gained good marks in most subjects, passed nine GCSEs with good grades and is studying Biology, Physics and Geography at A-level with Applied Maths A/S. Emma, like most teenagers, has boyfriends but she doesn't want to get into a long-term relationship since she thinks this would harm her studies. She like sports and outdoor activities, and she plays for the school football team as well as enjoying hockey and cross-country running. She is an avid Facebook fan, likes bands, dancing and goes to clubs whenever her parents let her. In common with several of her friends, Emma smokes, but doesn't think this is a problem.

Personae stimulate design exploration by providing a framework for thinking about how experiences might relate to different types of user, and how individual people might react to different designs [16]. More extreme personae (extreme characters [22]) can be useful for exploring new ideas for UE to escape from more conservative descriptions of user roles. Personae are part of audience analysis to describe the range of possible users, their goals and priorities. One problem which personae share with scenarios is the scope problem. More personae can empower design imagination; but it is far from clear when a 'necessary and sufficient' set of personae has been collected. Generally, the advice is to collect personae to represent each group of user stakeholders with an appropriate range of ages and gender.

STORYBOARDS

Scenarios and personae are inputs to stimulate design exploration. Storyboards are the initial outcomes of design, and may also be referred to as design sketches or wireframe models. The storyboard concept owes its origins to the cartoon industry in which ideas for cartoons were sketched as a series of drawings to illustrate key events in the storyline or script. Transferred to UI design, storyboards illustrate snapshots of interaction related to the users' tasks or script for the product (see Fig. 3.1).

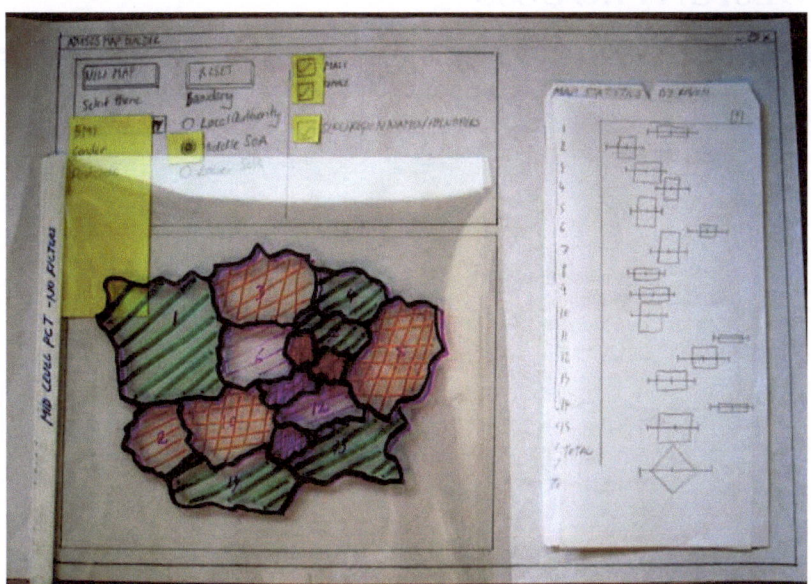

Figure 3.1: Storyboard mockup of a health informatics application illustrating different display options on maps and graphs.

Storyboards may be hand-drawn or prepared as PowerPoint animations or videos which are walked through following a script of how the product will be used. The walkthrough aims to elicit feedback from the users and focus discussion on critiquing and elaborating the design. One limitation of storyboards is that complex interactions are difficult to explain since interaction can only be represented by scripted animations or explained using paper materials. Ideas relating to interaction, immersion and presence which are often important parts of UE design can be difficult to illustrate with sketches and PowerPoint presentations. Nevertheless, storyboards do allow rapid iterative exploration of design ideas and can be gradually transformed into prototypes which allow more interactive functionality to be explained.

PROTOTYPES

This category includes a variety of design representations ranging from mockups/concept demonstrators with limited scripted functionality to partial software implementations that can demonstrate interaction and user experiences. The representations all result from the creative design process and illustrate concrete aspects of a design. The variation between the techniques lies in the media used (paper, video, computer media, interactive software), the cost of production, and the fidelity and extent of the representation of the intended design. The power of prototype lies in anchoring the focus of discussion in the concrete example and stimulating user reaction to specific features.

3.1   UE DESIGN PROCESS

The UE design process using on scenario-based design starts by establishing the users' high-level requirements and design goals, including priorities based on the UE criteria (see Fig. 3.2).

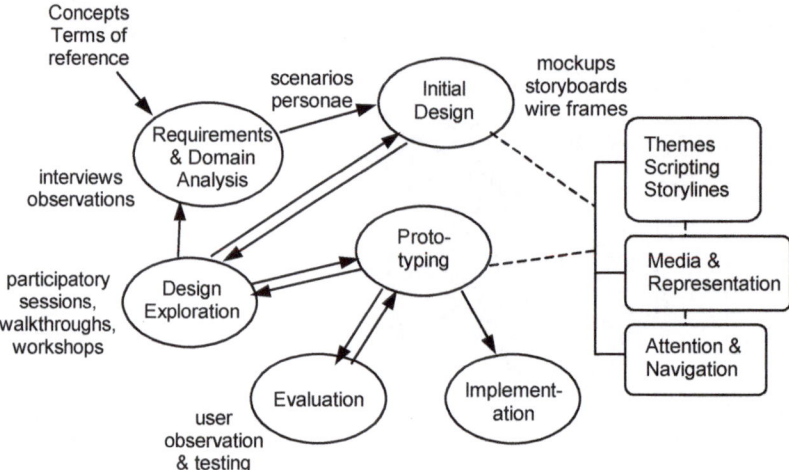

Figure 3.2: Summary of steps and techniques in the UE design process.

Scenarios and personae are collected or created to provide material for stimulating the design process. Creative brainstorming may be used to map out a space of ideas and concepts; once these have been prioritized, design realization becomes necessary to progress the user-designer dialogue. Design realizations are created in iterative cycles using scenarios and personae, possibly with examples of previous good designs for inspiration. Initial ideas lead to design exploration in which storyboards, wireframes or mockups are demonstrated to users in interview or workshop settings to get their feedback on the design and, more importantly, their contribution of ideas and participation in the design process. Representations of designs migrate through cycles of creation and evaluation with users as storyboards and early mockups are refined into prototypes. In prototyping, some commitment is made to software development. Prototypes tend to be evaluated with a more formal process of user testing following a task script to try out the product and debug the usability of the interaction design as well as assess aesthetics and other properties. After iterations of evaluation and prototyping, when the users are satisfied with the product or development money runs out, the decision to release a product is taken.

Three UE design activities apply to both initial design and prototyping. First is creating the high-level view of the sequence of interaction. In work/goal-oriented applications, this will follow a task model or use cases. Since task analysis and use case modelling of interactive sequences are covered in many HCI books [5, 56], I will not repeat the standard advice. Entertainment, education and more discretionary applications start with the high-level plan for interaction, commonly specified as storylines, narratives or scripts. For example, consider the following sources or inspiration that can come from drama [42]:

Settings: orient the audience to the purpose, location, time, and context.

Characters: (see personae) the actors are represented in the design as avatars; and how the audience of users can engage/interact with them.

Plot: how the story develops in phases composed of events, episodes and situations.

Movement: the pace at which the plot unfolds, related to flow.

Mood: how the emotional tone of interaction is manipulated by events and choice of media for pleasure, suspense, anxiety, fear, etc.

A good plot provides an initial setting then leads the audience through phases which build the story leading to the denouement or climax when the moral or purpose of the story becomes clear.

Progressive disclosure of facts and clues towards the denouement helps to maintain flow and engagement via suspense. The storyline can be planned using informal diagrams and sketches employing ideas from drama theory and trajectories [4] and experience planning techniques [12]. Trajectories are threads which describe journeys that actors (participants in the interaction) undergo, linking spaces, time, plot, roles and characters, as illustrated in Fig. 3.3. Multiple trajectories can be planned for different participants, with meetings. Roles can be interacting, or bystanders who observe but are not directly involved; and orchestrators which are power roles and can control others. Storyline scripting is illustrated in Fig. 3.3, showing the planned thread for the story with sketches of the interactive space, annotated with plans for mood and emotional responses.

An exploration game is illustrated, where the first player can get advice from the second player while following a trajectory through the virtual world, encountering active objects (clues) as well as surprise events. The storyline thread is linked to sketches giving detail of the graphical world and interactive effects. The extent of planning varies between designers; some may sketch ideas in detail although the majority tend to sketch in outline then mock up and prototype ideas.

One debate in the design and UX literature is the extent to which the process should be user-centred or design led. User-centred design can produce conservative solutions since users may

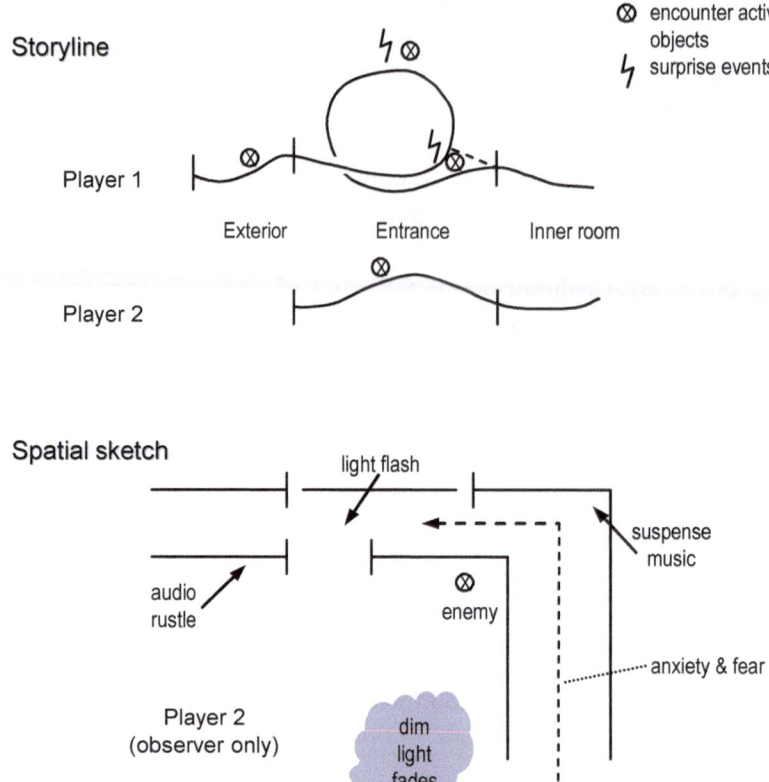

Figure 3.3: Storylines for planning interactive experience.

anchor their requirements and priorities on their previous experience rather than exploring new experiences. In contrast, designer-led exploration tends to develop fairly complete prototypes with the intent of expanding the envelope of UX. When products are being developed for new markets, design-led exploration may be more appropriate while for applications tailored to specific users and their tasks, a user-centred approach is advisable.

The second design consideration is selecting media and designing the interactive world. While media selection will be governed by the storyline and purpose of the application, it is also influenced by emotion and mood settings planned in the storyline. Media selection is also related to the third component, directing the user's attention. In more goal-oriented applications, attention needs to be directed to navigation cues and important content; in contrast, for entertainment and less task-oriented applications, attention controls are tools for emotion and mood manipulation. User attention may be stimulated to produce interest and curiosity in interaction or to mislead the user, thereby maintaining emotions of anxiety and suspense. Media selection and design for attention guidelines are given in the following section.

CHAPTER 4

Design Principles and Guidelines

Design advice for UE tends to be expressed as high-level and fairly general principles, accompanied by examples of good design employing the principle. This is not surprising since design for user engagement and experience will depend on the domain and details of who the users are and their goals. Many usability-oriented principles are already familiar in HCI (see [5, 50, 56, 60]) such as consistency in user interfaces, structured layout and exhortations to consider human cognitive limitations, such as working memory. There is no point in repeating this advice in this chapter, so I will concentrate on UE design principles which only appear in the visual, graphical and interaction design literature [40, 45, 48]. The source of most of the following guidelines can be found in Lidwell et al. [45]; where the origins are elsewhere the source is referenced.

Many guidelines are explained more effectively by illustration than descriptive text; however, illustrating each guideline would have resulted in a book rather than one chapter. Therefore, I have added an appendix which illustrates several designs and points out where good design has resulted from application of the guidelines and poor design has appeared in their absence.

IMMERSION AND PRESENCE

As explained in Chapter 2, both creating an avatar for the user and providing a 3D world in which to interact provide immersion and a better sense of presence. Presence can be enhanced by adding audio in 3D, and haptic feedback. Social presence is enhanced by richer communication media, providing more information about people being conversed with, and social awareness functions, such as newsfeeds found on social networking sites.

FLOW IN INTERACTION

Besides creating interesting storylines and controlling the optimal balance between challenge and ease of operation, there are other design principles which contribute to flow and natural interaction although these require considerable interpretation and design expertise to realize in specific applications:

Affordances: the shape of an object naturally suggests how it can be manipulated and used, including clues to its functionality. Classic affordances are the shape of door handles which suggest either turning, pushing or pulling actions to open the door. The extent to which affordances rely on learned common sense knowledge as opposed to naturally suggestibility of shapes is an open question.

Metaphors: shapes and graphical structures which either suggest organization or possible actions. Metaphors may either directly suggest groups, categories of objects, or actions, or provide the context in which action and functionality of components is suggested, e.g., a palette metaphor in a graphics package suggests the functionality and actions that are possible with the paint brush, eraser, pencil, icons, etc. Metaphors and affordances are closely related. Both metaphors and affordances help 'recognition rather than recall' and 'natural mappings' by providing memory cues to suggest actions from common sense knowledge and analogical memory.

SELECTING AND DESIGNING MEDIA FOR MOOD AND AROUSAL

Dynamic media: (video, speech) are generally more arousing because we find stimuli which changes and is harder to ignore than static images or text.

Natural images: such as landscapes have calming effects and tend to reduce our arousal; in contrast, images of designed artefacts and unusual objects, e.g., space rockets, stimulate our curiosity and tend to be arousing.

Sounds from nature: audio has a similar effect; the sound of wind in trees, water and waves calm while the noise of racing cars and aircraft arouses.

Unusual or challenging images: for example, Dali and surrealist painters created unusual images that disobeyed normal laws of form and perspective to stimulate the users' imagination and increase attraction.

Depth of field: layering in images and use of 3D effects promotes interest and curiosity more than simple 2D representations.

Oddity: when one or more elements in a large image don't fit, this invokes cognitive dissonance or our natural ability to spot the irregular among the regular. Oddity effects often disobey Gestalt principles; see also aesthetic appeal. Oddity can be used to stimulate curiosity and increase arousal.

SELECTING MEDIA TO ATTRACT AND PERSUADE

Photographs of people: attract attention especially when the person is looking directly at the user; see also dynamic media: gaze) [58].

Faces of average people and baby faces: faces which represent the norm in a population (Mr/Ms average) and young children are more attractive. We are very susceptible to the large-eyes effect in young animals, as exploited by Disney cartoons.

Polite praise: use of please, thank you, and simple compliments like "that was an excellent choice" increase people's tendency to judge the computer as pleasant and enjoyable.

For more detailed treatment of design for persuasive technology, see [28].

SELECTING MEDIA FOR EMOTIONAL EFFECTS

Dangerous and threatening episodes: e.g., being chased by a tiger, gory images (mutilated body) and erotic content all increase arousal and invoke emotions ranging from fear to anger whereas pleasant images (e.g., flowers, sunset) tend to decrease it, i.e., have calming effects and produce pleasurable emotions responses [58].

Characters: characters can appear threatening or benevolent depending on their appearance or dress, e.g., disfigured people appear threatening and evoke emotions ranging from fear to disgust. Characters familiar from popular culture can be used for emotional effect.

Dialogue: spoken dialogue is probably the most powerful tool for creating emotional responses, from threats to empathy. Emotional effects are additive so choice of character with a threatening appearance, complemented by a menacing voice tone and an aggressive dialogue, all reinforce the emotions of anxiety and fear.

Music: can set the appropriate mood, e.g., loud strident pieces will arouse and excite, romantic music calms and invokes pleasure, etc.

SELECTING AND DESIGNING MEDIA TO ATTRACT ATTENTION

Dynamic media: such as video, speech and audio all attract attention. Indeed, any change in an image also stimulates attention; however, we rapidly become used to the new stimulus so attention effects wane. Images of people with their *gaze* directed at the user are another effective choice for drawing attention since this mimics human attention in the real world.

Visual salience: pictures attract attention in preference to text; within images and text, attention-grabbing stimuli in order of salience are any change (blink, move), oddity effects using colour contrast, shape or size.

DESIGN FOR AESTHETIC APPEAL

Judicious use of *colour*: colour use should be balanced and low saturation pastel colours should be used for backgrounds. Designs should not use more than 2-3 fully saturated intense colours. Yellow is salient for alerting, red/green have danger/safety positive/negative associations, and blue is more effective for background. Low saturated colours (pale shades with white) have a calming effect and are also useful for backgrounds. Colour is a complex subject in its own right; for more guidance, see Travis [70].

Gestalt effects: there are several visual patterns (see Fig. 4.1) which we recognize and interpret instinctively that are collective known as 'Gestalt' effects in perceptual psychology:

Closure: we naturally see the complete object such as a circle, even if it is not complete.

Good continuation: items organized in a visual sequence or on a curve are perceived to be related or belong to a structure.

Similarity: objects which share visual attributes (colour, size, shape) will be seen as a category or group.

Proximity: objects which are placed close together and separate from others are perceived as a group.

Präganz: the tendency to ascribe meaning to images based on similarity to images we remember.

Symmetry: symmetrical visual layouts, e.g., bilateral, radial or rotational organization that can be folded over to show the symmetrical match, have pleasing effects.

Figure ground: the juxtaposition of visual features or grouping of shapes causes higher-order structures to emerge from the image. This effect can be used with verbal priming to create surprise when the structure is not immediately apparent.

Depth of field: use of layers in an image stimulates interest and can attract by promoting curiosity. Use of background image with low saturated colour provides depth for foreground components.

Use of shape: use of curved shapes conveys an attractive visual style, in contrast to blocks and rectangles which portray structure, categories and order in a layout.

Visual structure and organization: dividing an image into thirds (Right, Centre, Left or Top, Middle, Bottom) provides an attractive visual organization while rectangular shapes following the golden ratio (height/width =1.618) are aesthetically pleasing.

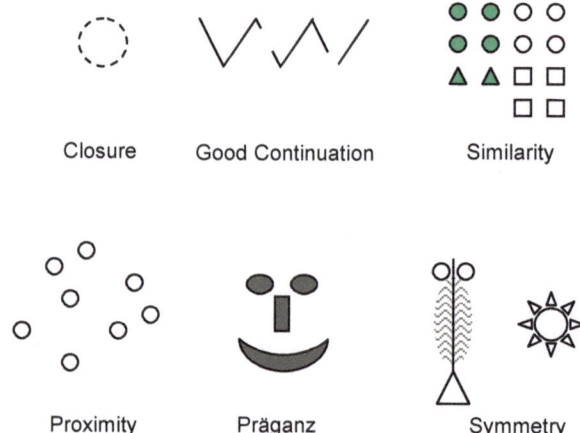

Figure 4.1: Gestalt Visualization.

Although guidelines can provide ideas that can improve aesthetic design and the attractiveness of interfaces, they are no guarantee that these effects will be achieved. Design is often a tradeoff between ease of use and aesthetic design; for instance, use of progressive disclosure to promote flow may well be perceived as being difficult to learn by others. Visual effects often show considerable individual differences and learning effects, so a well intentioned design might not be successful. The advice, as with most design, is test ideas and preliminary designs with users to check interpretations, critique ideas and evaluate their acceptability.

CHAPTER 5

Perspectives and Conclusions

This chapter set out to explain user experience in terms of the psychology of interaction. A design process was described, cross-referenced to guidelines to provide ideas for particular design topics. However, following the caveat I noted in the introduction, the reader should be aware that there is no substitute for experience. UE design requires considerable interpretation of how to design for a particular context. The contextualist school of UX [23, 46] argue that experience can only be analyzed by deep understanding of the context of use. Meaning and feelings only arise from the interaction; in other words, how a person understands the act of interaction; hence, experience arises from interaction in a specific context. For example, critical perspectives from post-modern humanities research might be applied to interpret aesthetic experience [2]. While I agree that interaction and use arise from our abilities as intelligent primates to make use of tools in novel ways, and that much experience can not be predicted by designers, this does not mean we should shy away from trying to understand user experience in detail and, when our understanding matures, predict experiences in contexts which share broad similarities. That is the aim of this chapter although I acknowledge there is a long way to go to define the laws governing "contexts with broad similarities."

Furthermore, design is invariably a trade-off between conflicting demands while processes and guidelines imply that a "cookbook" solution is possible by following the rules. The reason for including considerable background to UE from cognitive psychology is to give some knowledge that can help interpretation of the guidelines and process advice given in Chapters 3 and 4. Good design arises from a process of hard work, knowledge and experience.

In the wider view, user experience and engagement can be interpreted at several levels, most of which are represented by other chapters in this book. I take what is described by some as a cognitivist or positivist viewpoint in that I believe in detailed explanations and, where possible, predictive theories about how people behave, and advocate that such theories can be applied to design. Furthermore, I believe that knowledge can be captured and reused that will, with enlightened interpretation, produce design quality when applied to a wide range of applications. This view puts me at odds with interaction design researchers [30, 59] who argue that design expertise can only be produced by several years of education and mentoring. In extremis, I agree; however, design schools only produce a small number of graduates each year, yet the demand for UX design vastly exceeds the supply of such expertise. Methodical advice coupled with less intensive training is the only way out of the skills bottleneck.

I share a cognitivist view with Marc Hassenzahl, who also searches for general and predictive theories, as well as methods for quantifying users' evaluation of aesthetics and other attributes of user experience. Hassenzahl's quest is to find the deep-seated underlying constructs which we all use to assess user experience, i.e., pragmatics, hedonics, and goodness, even though we might not be consciously aware of such ideas. While I believe this quest is valuable, as Andrew Monk points out, we have to be aware of variation in evaluation across a variation of people and products so we can establish the general truth of such constructs through a thorough analysis [47]. I diverge with Hassenzahl and the rival "cognitive" ontology of users' experience from Noam Tractinsky (expressive and classic aesthetics, etc.); in that, I believe user judgement is more contextually based in tasks and prior knowledge. Much of my work with Antonella de Angeli and Jan Hartmann has been directed toward a cognitive theory that aims, ultimately, to predict contextual effects on user judgement of UE. So far, we have demonstrated that user judgement is, indeed, very pliable, thus questioning the value of general constructs such as hedonics without placing them in a model of the decision-making process.

Peter Wright and John McCarthy might argue that my quest, and, indeed, Marc Hassenzahl's, is doomed to failure since user experience can only be understood and evaluated by individuals in a context, to which I reply that contextualization of evaluation results in a nihilism of the specific that hinders attempts to generalize theory. They would point to interpretive theorizing (e.g., using [20]) and generalization of heuristics from reflection over numerous case studies and experience. My riposte is that heuristics and reflection have a weak leverage on design in comparison to my guidelines and model; furthermore, they can not enable quantitative comparisons of UE between products as delivered by Hassenzahl's AttrakDIF questionnaires. Ironically, my research on contextual influences on user judgement of UE might be seen as a move, albeit tangentially, in McCarthy and Wright's direction. They may assert that as my research continues, I will find more detailed contextual influence on user judgement and interactions between the influences; consequently, I may drown in the complexity of context, so I would be better advised to join their contextual camp. My view is that understanding complexity is worth the effort. I would also challenge them to unpack in a systematic manner just what they mean by context, so we might converge on a middle ground of where it is profitable to formalize knowledge and where it is better left open to human interpretation. Finally, I can rest assured that readers will draw their own conclusions, based on cognitive processes with which I am familiar. What would be more interesting is to gather the readers' opinions on how these different approaches contribute towards design. Maybe, there is a challenge for the publisher to enhance user experience of the printed word.

APPENDIX A

Website Design Examples

A.1 NIKE WEBSITE

This site produced a positive user experience and was well rated on Tractinsky aesthetics scales citebib67. The good design features which illustrate application of the guidelines: (a) design of animations to tell a story and thereby induce the sense of flow; animations unfold in a sequence (man running, birds flying, etc.) related to a theme of motion; (b) use of natural images and depth of field; (c) open savannah-like landscapes; and (d) animation to attract attention: after the introductory animations finished the menu options at the base of the screen were highlighted.

http://www.morganclaypool.com/page/sutcliffe

A.2   INTELLIPAGE WEBSITE

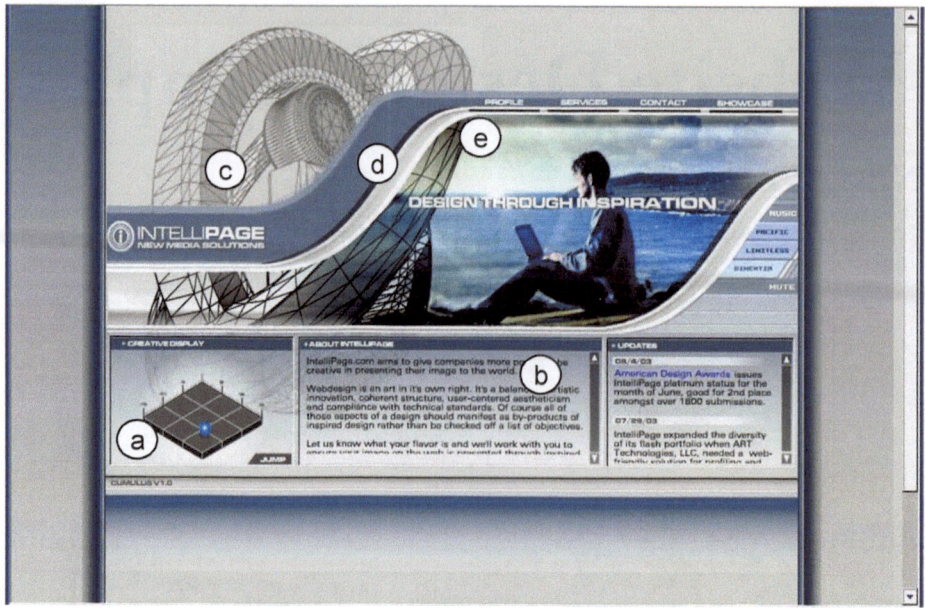

This site also made extensive use of animation: (a) pin ball game, (b) text, and (c) background (see video) to attract attention as well as using images and depth of field to interest the user. Shape is used for aesthetic effect, (d); with depth of field (e). In contrast to Nike, the animations were not thematically designed as a story; furthermore, animations were running concurrently, which distracted attention. User ratings on aesthetic scales and overall preference were significantly lower than for Nike [67].

http://www.morganclaypool.com/page/sutcliffe

A.3   BBC NEWS WEBSITE

The BBC website is frequently cited as an example of good design. Content is an important criterion for this site, so the more traditional block structure helps with navigation (a) since usability is probably more important than aesthetics. The site uses animation in a ticker banner headline to attract attention (b), as well as including many images to interest the viewer (c).

A.4   BBC INTERACTIVE WEBSITE: BIG AL DINOSAUR GAME

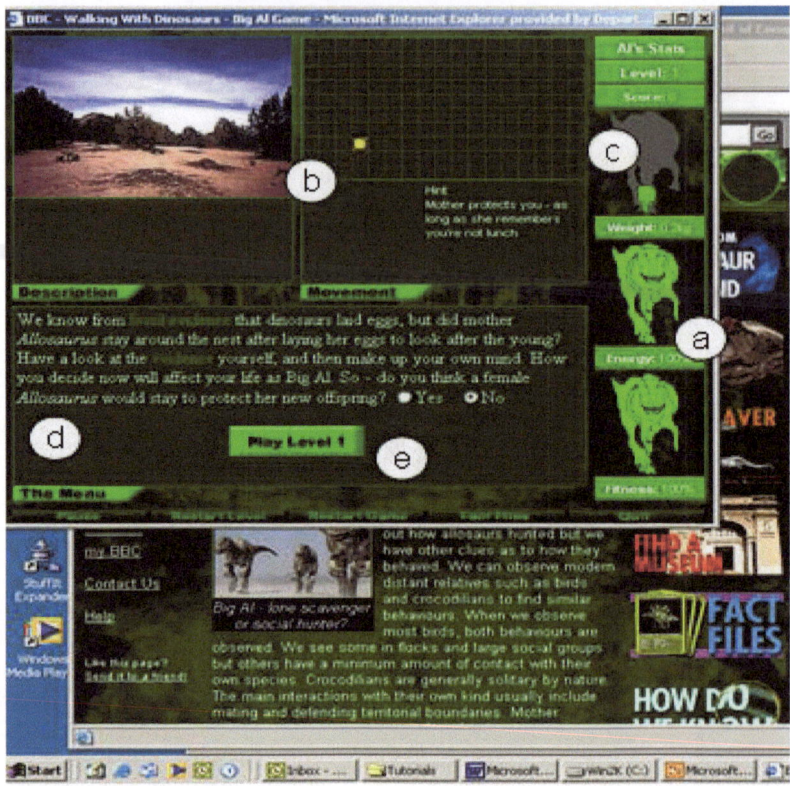

Other parts of the BBC site, (above figure) are designed for more direct engagement where the user can explore scientific topics using a games format. The design promotes presence by giving the user an identity (a) in the game (pick a dinosaur); a virtual environment to move in (b); and feedback on their progress (c); as well as explanations for the success or failure of their actions (d). This design gives a good sense of flow (see skill-level setting (e)) and engagement in spite of the limited graphics and interactive controls (arrow keys).

A.5   JUMP TOMORROW: ENTRY PAGE AND INTERACTIVE MAP

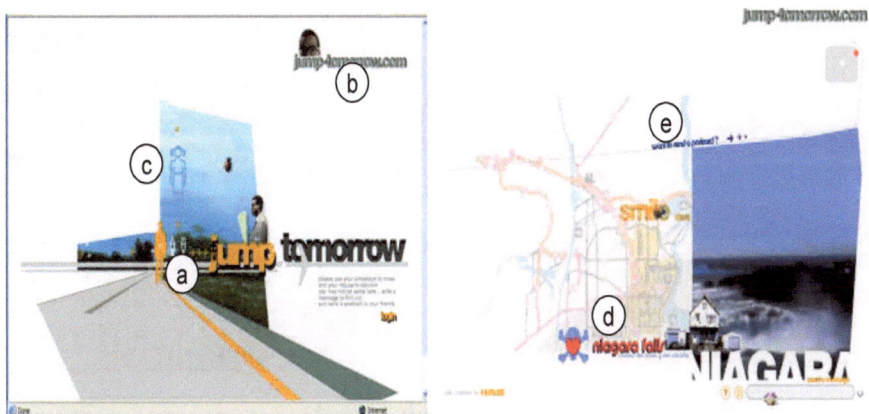

Jump Tomorrow was a film publicity website for a somewhat quirky film which is reflected in the website. The site was engaging for some users but intensely frustrating for others, illustrating a trade-off between poor usability and aesthetics. Shape, colour, white space and depth of field (a) promoted an aesthetic look and feel while oddity in visual design stimulated curiosity (b). The user had to choose a character (c: boy/girl) and then their presence was indicated by a bee. As the user traversed a landscape (d), odd effects would pop up, showing images from the film, and promoting engagement by interaction (e) such as e-mailing a postcard (from the film) to a friend. For users who became engaged, the design promoted flow by unpredictable effects and emotions of surprise and fun, in reaction to the strange images. A journey could be followed leading to scenes from the film, so the design was scripted with a trajectory in mind. However, users who did not understand the interactive metaphor found the site intensely frustrating.

A.6   VIRGIN ATLANTIC WEBSITE: DESIGN EVOLUTION

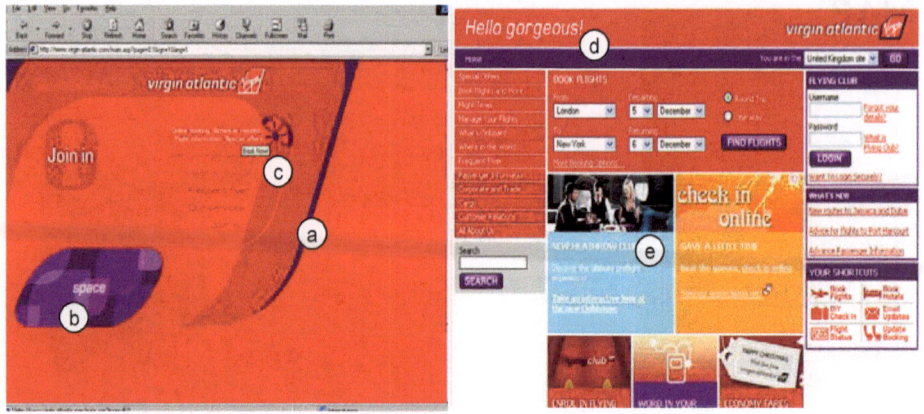

The left half of the figure shows the Virgin Atlantic website splash page in 2002. This design used colour for aesthetic appeal as well as promoting the brand and corporate identity. Curved shapes (a) gave an aesthetic look while animations in the window (b) stimulated interest and curiosity. Mouse over pop-up menus and text (c) used to change, to attract attention and unfolding parts of the site to maintain interest. The site was rated to be more interesting and aesthetically designed than rival airlines at the time [62] and illustrates successful investment in aesthetic design. The design did not last and was replaced by a more functionally oriented, less interesting design, shown on the right of the figure although personal messages (d) and image (e) are still used to attract the user.

A.7   SECOND LIFE E-COMMERCE VIRTUAL WORLD

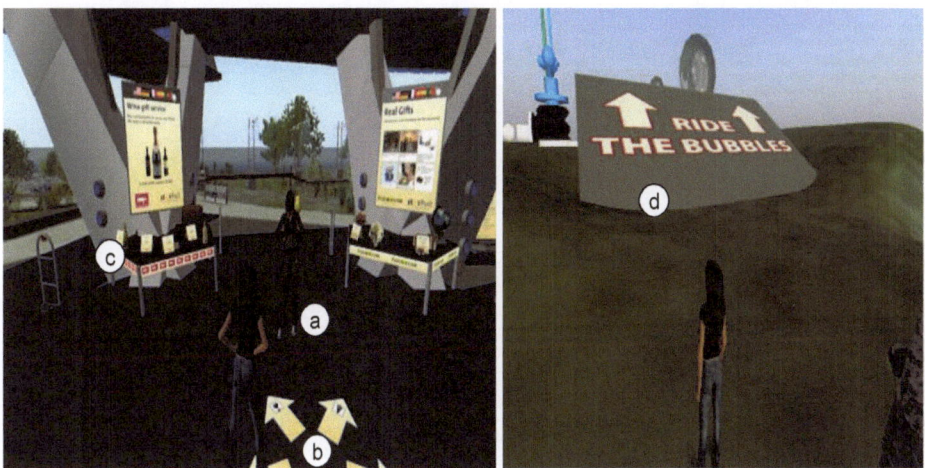

Second Life illustrates design for presence using virtual characters and a rich 3D graphical environment. Users can move their avatar (a) by walking or flying for large distances (b), so they can adjust the flow of their interaction. Communication is possible by voice, so combined with the graphical world, this gives a good sense of social presence. Avatar faces can be controlled to gaze and show simple facial expressions thus affording attraction and attention control. Engagement is promoted by interaction; you can go shopping (c), ride a horse, go sailing and indulge yourself in a host of semi-realistic activities. In the second figure, engagement and flow have been enhanced by special interactive effects; flying the bubble (d) takes the users on a fly-through journey of a particular site. The sense of immersion comes from interacting through your own (avatar) presence. Users can purchase islands and design their own avatars and interactive world, so customization and ownership can be an important UX criterion for some users; however, most users pay for the design of their island/ buildings, etc., and purchase avatars and their clothes, so it appears that customization is only important for a minority. In the video, a virtual degree ceremony is illustrated in which overseas students are virtually present and receive their degrees.

http://www.morganclaypool.com/page/sutcliffe

Bibliography

[1] Baddeley, A. D. 1986. *Working memory.* Oxford: Oxford University Press.

[2] Bardzell, J. 2008. Interaction criticism and aesthetics. *Proceedings: CHI 2009: 27th International Conference on Human Factors in Computing Systems, Boston*, pp. 2357–2366. New York: ACM Press. DOI: 10.1145/1518701.1519063

[3] Beck, K. 1999. *Extreme programming explained: Embracing change.* New York: Addison-Wesley.

[4] Benford, S., Giannachi, G., Koleva, B., and Rodden, T. 2009. From interaction to trajectories: Designing coherent journeys through user experiences. *Proceedings: CHI 2009: 27th International Conference on Human Factors in Computing Systems, Boston*, pp. 709–718. New York: ACM Press. DOI: 10.1145/1518701.1518812

[5] Benyon, D., Turner, P., and Turner, S. 2004. *Designing interactive systems: People, activities, contexts, technologies.* Reading MA: Addison Wesley.

[6] Berlyne, D. E. 1960. *Conflict, arousal, and curiosity.* New York: McGraw-Hill. DOI: 10.1037/11164-000

[7] Bloch, P. 1995. Seeking the ideal form: Product design and consumer response. *Journal of Marketing,* **59**, 16–29. DOI: 10.2307/1252116

[8] Blythe, M. A., Overbeeke, K., Monk, A. F., and Wright, P. C. 2004. *Funology: From usability to enjoyment.* Boston MA: Kluwer.

[9] Bolchini, D., Garzotto, F., and Sorce. S. 2009. Does branding need Web usability? A value-oriented empirical study. *Proceedings of INTERACT 2009*, pp. 652–665. Berlin: Springer. DOI: 10.1007/978-3-642-03658-3_70

[10] Brennan, S. E., and Clark, H. H. 1996. Conceptual pacts and lexical choice of conversation. *Journal of Experimental Psychology: Learning, Memory and Cognition,* **22**, pp. 1482–93. DOI: 10.1037/0278-7393.22.6.1482

[11] Buxton, B. 2007. *Sketching user experiences: Getting the design right and the right design.* Amsterdam: Elsevier.

[12] Callele, D., Neufeld, E., and Schneider, K. 2006. Emotional requirements in video games. *Proceedings: 14th IEEE International Requirements Engineering Conference RE06*, pp. 299–302. Los Alamitos CA: IEEE Computer Society Press. DOI: 10.1109/RE.2006.19

[13] Carroll, J. M. 2000. *Making use: Scenario-based design of human-computer interactions*. Cambridge MA: MIT Press.

[14] Carroll, J. M. (Ed.) 1995. *Scenario-based design: Envisioning work and technology in system development*. New York: Wiley.

[15] Clark, H. H. 1996. *Using language*. Cambridge: Cambridge University Press.

[16] Cooper, A., Reimann, R., and Cronin, D. 2007. *About face 3: The essentials of interaction design*. Indianapolis: Wiley.

[17] Csikszentmihalyi, M. 2002. *Flow: The classic work on how to achieve happiness* Revised ed. London: Rider.

[18] De Angeli, A., and Brahnam, S. 2008. I hate you! Disinhibition with virtual partners. *Interacting with Computers*, **20**, pp. 302–310. DOI: 10.1016/j.intcom.2008.02.004

[19] De Angeli, A., Sutcliffe, A. G., and Hartmann, J. 2006. Interaction, usability and aesthetics: What influences users' preferences? *Proceedings: Conference on Designing Interactive Systems, DIS-06*, pp. 271–280. New York: ACM Press. DOI: 10.1145/1142405.1142446

[20] Dewey, J. 1934. Art as experience (reprinted paperback edition, 2009.) New York: Perigee Books.

[21] Dion, K., Berscheid, E., and Walster, E. 1972. What is beautiful is good. *Journal of Personality and Social Psychology*, **24**, pp. 285–290. DOI: 10.1037/h0033731

[22] Djajadiningrat, J. P., Gaver, W. W., and Frens, J. W. 2000. Interaction relabelling and extreme characters: Methods for exploring aesthetic interactions. In D. Boyarski, and W. A. Kellogg, Eds. *Conference Proceedings: DIS2000 Designing Interactive Systems: Processes, Practices Methods and Techniques, New York 17-19 August 2000*, pp. 66–71. New York: ACM Press. DOI: 10.1145/347642.347664

[23] Dourish, P. 2004. *Where the action is: The foundations of embodied interaction*. Cambridge MA: MIT Press.

[24] DSDM. 1995. *DSDM Consortium: Dynamic Systems Development Method*. Farnham Surrey: Tesseract Publishers.

[25] Dunbar, R. 2002. Modelling primate behavioral ecology. *International Journal of Primatology*, **23**, pp. 785–819. DOI: 10.1023/A:1015576915296

[26] Fischer, G. 2001. User modeling in human-computer interaction. *User Modeling and User-Adapted Interaction*, **11**, pp. 65–86. DOI: 10.1023/A:1011145532042

[27] Fischer, G., Giaccardi, E., Ye, Y., Sutcliffe, A. G., and Mehandjiev, N. 2004. A framework for end-user development: Socio-technical perspectives and meta-design. *Communications of the ACM*, **47**, pp. 33–39. DOI: 10.1145/1015864.1015884

[28] Fogg, B. J. 2003. *Persuasive technology: Using computers to change what we think and do*. San Francisco: Morgan Kaufmann.

[29] Forlizzi, J., and Battarbee, K. 2004. Understanding experience in interactive systems. *Proceedings: 2004 Conference on Designing Interactive Systems DIS 04*, p. 261. New York: ACM Press. DOI: 10.1145/1013115.1013152

[30] Gaver, W. W., Beaver, J., and Benford, S. 2003. Ambiguity as a resource for design. In V. Bellotti, T. Erickson, G. Cockton, and P. Korhonen, Eds. *CHI 2003 Conference Proceedings: Conference on Human Factors in Computing Systems, Fort Lauderdale FL 5-10 April 2003*, pp. 233–240. New York: ACM Press.

[31] Green, W. S., and Jordan, P. W. 2001. *Pleasure with products: Beyond usability*. London: Taylor and Francis.

[32] Hartmann, J., Sutcliffe, A. G., and De Angeli, A. 2007. Investigating attractiveness in web user interfaces. *Proceedings: CHI-07, San Jose*, New York: ACM Press. DOI: 10.1145/1240624.1240687

[33] Hartmann, J., Sutcliffe, A. G., and De Angeli, A. 2008. Towards a theory of user judgement of aesthetics and user interface quality. *ACM Transactions on Computer-Human Interaction*, **15**. DOI: 10.1145/1460355.1460357

[34] Hassenzahl, M. 2004. The interplay of beauty, goodness and usability in interactive products. *Human-Computer Interaction*, **19**, pp. 319–349. DOI: 10.1207/s15327051hci1904_2

[35] Hassenzahl, M., Schöbel, M., and Trautmann, T. 2008. How motivational orientation influences the evaluation and choice of hedonic and pragmatic interactive products: The role of regulatory focus. *Interacting with Computers*, **20**, pp. 473–479. DOI: 10.1016/j.intcom.2008.05.001

[36] Hassenzahl, M., and Tractinsky, N. 2006. User experience: A research agenda. *Behaviour and Information Technology*, **25**, pp. 91–97.

[37] Ince, S. 2006. *Writing for video games*. London: Methuen.

[38] ISO. 1995. *ISO 13407: Human-centred design processes for interactive systems*. International Standards Organisation.

[39] ISO. 1997. *ISO 9241: Ergonomic requirements for office systems with visual display terminals VDTs*. International Standards Organisation.

[40] Kristof, R., and Satran, A. 1995. *Interactivity by design: Creating and communicating with new media*. Mountain View CA: Adobe Press.

[41] Kyng, M. 1995. Creating contexts for design. In J. M. Carroll, Ed., *Scenario based design*, pp. 85–108. Chichester: Wiley.

[42] Laurel, B. 1991. *Computers as theatre*. Reading MA: Addison Wesley

[43] Lavie, T., and Tractinsky, N. 2004. Assessing dimensions of perceived visual aesthetics of web sites. *International Journal of Human-Computer Studies*, **60**, pp. 269–298. DOI: 10.1016/j.ijhcs.2003.09.002

[44] Law, E. L., Roto, V., Hassenzahl, M., Vermeeren, A. P. O., and Kort, J. 2009. Understanding, scoping and defining user experience: A survey approach. *Proceedings: CHI 2009, Boston MA*, pp. 719–728. DOI: 10.1145/1518701.1518813

[45] Lidwell, W., Holden K., and Butler, J. 2003. *Universal principles of design*. Gloucester MA: Rockport.

[46] McCarthy, J., and Wright, P. 2005. *Technology as experience*. Cambridge MA: MIT Press.

[47] Monk, A.F. 2004. The product as a fixed-effect asset fallacy. *Human-Computer Interaction*, **19**, pp. 371–375. DOI: 10.1207/s15327051hci1904_6

[48] Mullet, K., and Sano, D. 1995. *Designing visual interfaces: Communication oriented techniques*. Englewood Cliffs NJ: SunSoft Press.

[49] Neisser, U. 1976. *Cognition and reality*. San Francisco: W.H. Freeman.

[50] Nielsen, J. 1993. *Usability engineering*. Boston MA: Academic Press.

[51] Norman, D. A. 1988. *The psychology of everyday things*. New York: Basic Books.

[52] Norman, D. A. 2004. *Emotional design: Why we love or hate everyday things*. New York: Basic Books.

[53] Ortony, A., Clore, G. L., and Collins, A. 1988. *The cognitive structure of emotions*. Cambridge: Cambridge University Press.

[54] Payne, J. W., Bettman, J. R., and Johnson, E. J. 1993. *The adaptive decision maker*. Cambridge: Cambridge University Press.

[55] Petty, R. E., and Cacioppo, J. T. 1986. The elaboration likelihood model of persuasion. *Advances in Experimental Social Psychology*, **19**, pp. 123–205. DOI: 10.1016/S0065-2601(08)60214-2

[56] Preece, J., Rogers, Y., and Sharp, H. 2007. *Interaction design: Beyond human computer interaction* 2nd ed. Chichester: Wiley.

[57] Rasmussen, J. 1986. *Information processing in human computer interaction: An approach to cognitive engineering*. Amsterdam: North Holland.

[58] Reeves, B., and Nass, C. 1996. *The media equation: How people treat computers, television and new media like real people and places*. Stanford CA/Cambridge: CLSI/Cambridge University Press.

[59] Sengers P. 2004. The engineering of experience. In M. A. Blythe, K. Overbeeke, A. F. Monk, and P. C. Wright Eds., *Funology: From usability to enjoyment* pp. 19–30. Boston MA: Kluwer.

[60] Shneiderman, B., and Plaisant, C. 2004. *Designing the user interface: Strategies for effective interaction* 4th ed. Reading MA: Addison-Wesley.

[61] Short, J., Williams, E., and Christie, B. 1976. *The social psychology of telecommunications*. Chichester: Wiley.

[62] Sutcliffe, A. G. 2002. Assessing the reliability of heuristic evaluation for website attractiveness and usability. *Proceedings HICSS-35: Hawaii International Conference on System Sciences, Hawaii 7-10 January 2002*, pp. 1838–1847. Los Alamitos, CA: IEEE Computer Society Press. DOI: 10.1109/HICSS.2002.994098

[63] Sutcliffe, A. G., and Carroll, J. M. 1998. Generalizing claims and reuse of HCI knowledge. In H. Johnson, L. Nigay, and C. Roast, Eds. *People and Computers XIII; Proceedings: BCS-HCI Conference, Sheffield 1-4 September 1998*, pp. 159–176. Berlin: Springer.

[64] Sutcliffe, A. G., and DeAngeli, A. 2005. Assessing interaction styles in web user interfaces. In M. F. Costabile, and F. Paterno, Eds. *Proceedings: Human Computer Interaction - Interact 2005, Rome*, pp. 405–417. Berlin: Springer. DOI: 10.1007/11555261_34

[65] Sutcliffe, A. G., Fickas, S., and Sohlberg, M. 2005. Personal and contextual requirements engineering. *Proceedings: 13th IEEE International Conference on Requirements Engineering, Paris 29 August - 2 September 2005*, pp. 19–28. Los Alamitos CA: IEEE Computer Society Press. DOI: 10.1109/RE.2005.51

[66] Sutcliffe, A. G., Gault, B., and Shin, J. E. 2005. Presence, memory and interaction in virtual environments. *International Journal of Human-Computer Studies*, **62**, pp. 307–327. DOI: 10.1016/j.ijhcs.2004.11.010

[67] Sutcliffe, A. G., and Namoune, A. 2008. Getting the message across: Visual attention, aesthetic design and what users remember. *Proceedings: DIS-08, Cape Town*, pp. 11–19. New York: ACM Press. DOI: 10.1145/1394445.1394447

[68] Thomas, P., and Macredie, R. D. 2002. Introduction to the new usability. *ACM Transactions on Computer-Human Interaction*, **9**, pp. 69–73. DOI: 10.1145/513665.513666

[69] Tractinsky, N. 1997. Aesthetics and apparent usability: Empirically assessing cultural and methodological issues. In Pemberton S. Ed., *Human Factors in Computing Systems: CHI 97 Conference Proceedings, Atlanta GA 22-27 May 1997*, pp. 115–122. New York: ACM Press. DOI: 10.1145/258549

[70] Travis, D. 1991. *Effective colour displays: Theory and practice*. Boston MA: Academic Press.

[71] Witmer, B. G., and Singer, M. J. 1999. Measuring presence in virtual environments: A presence questionnaire. *Presence*, **7**, pp. 225–240.

Author's Biography

ALISTAIR SUTCLIFFE

Alistair Sutcliffe is Professor of Systems Engineering in the Manchester Business School, University of Manchester. He has been principal investigator on fifteen EPSRC and European Union projects on requirements engineering, multimedia user interfaces, safety critical systems and cognitive modelling for information retrieval. Currently funded research projects include EPSRC/ESRC Developing Theory for Evolving Socio-technical Systems (TESS), which is investigating technology-mediated social and work relationships based on Dunbar's Social Brain Theory; EPSRC e-Science project ADaptive VISualisation tools for E-Science collaboration (ADVISES), which is producing interactive visualization tools for health informatics researchers; and EPSRC Artificial Cultures, which is researching evolutionary computing simulations for complex socio-technical systems. His research interests span a wide area within human computer interaction and software engineering. In HCI particular interests are interaction theory, and user interface design methods for the web, multimedia, and safety-critical systems; application of cognitive theory to design, and design of complex socio-technical systems. In software engineering, he specializes in requirements engineering methods and tools, scenario-based design, knowledge reuse and theories of domain knowledge. Alistair Sutcliffe is a leading member of both the international HCI and requirements engineering communities. He serves on the editorial boards of *ACM-TOCHI*, *REJ* and *JASE*. He is founder of IFIP TC-13 Working Group 13.2 *Methodology for User-Centred Design* and a member of IFIP working groups 8.1 (*Information Systems*) and 2.9 (*Requirements Engineering*) and is the editor of the ISO standard 14915, on *Multimedia user interface design*. He has over 200 publications, including five books, and several edited volumes of papers. He was awarded the IFIP Silver Core in 2000.